I0794784

Counseling and Discipleship Journal

This journal belongs to

P&R
PUBLISHING
P.O. BOX 817 • PHILLIPSBURG • NEW JERSEY 08865-0817

Have any feedback on this journal?
Write to P&R at editorial@prpbooks.com with your comments.
We'd love to hear from you.

ISBN: 978-1-62995-641-1 (pbk)

Printed in the United States of America

Contents

Counseling Notes
Session 1

Date:
Location:

Growth Assignments for Session 1:

Scripture for Memorization:

Session 2 Date:

Session 2 Location:

Growth Assignments and Additional Notes

Growth Assignments and Additional Notes

Counseling Notes
Session 2

Date:
Location:

Growth Assignments for Session 2:

Scripture for Memorization:

Session 3 Date:

Session 3 Location:

Growth Assignments and Additional Notes

Growth Assignments and Additional Notes

Counseling Notes
Session 3

Date:
Location:

Growth Assignments for Session 3:

Scripture for Memorization:

Session 4 Date:

Session 4 Location:

Growth Assignments and Additional Notes

Growth Assignments and Additional Notes

Counseling Notes | Date:

Session 4 | Location:

Growth Assignments for Session 4:

Scripture for Memorization:

Session 5 Date:

Session 5 Location:

Growth Assignments and Additional Notes

Growth Assignments and Additional Notes

Counseling Notes
Session 5

Date:
Location:

Growth Assignments for Session 5:

Scripture for Memorization:

Session 6 Date:

Session 6 Location:

Growth Assignments and Additional Notes

Growth Assignments and Additional Notes

Counseling Notes
Session 6

Date:
Location:

Growth Assignments for Session 6:

Scripture for Memorization:

Session 7 Date:

Session 7 Location:

Growth Assignments and Additional Notes

Growth Assignments and Additional Notes

Counseling Notes
Session 7

Date:
Location:

Growth Assignments for Session 7:

Scripture for Memorization:

Session 8 Date:

Session 8 Location:

Growth Assignments and Additional Notes

Counseling Notes
Session 8

Date:
Location:

Growth Assignments for Session 8:

Scripture for Memorization:

Session 9 Date:

Session 9 Location:

Growth Assignments and Additional Notes

Counseling Notes
Session 9

Date:
Location:

Growth Assignments for Session 9:

Scripture for Memorization:

Session 10 Date:

Session 10 Location:

Growth Assignments and Additional Notes

Counseling Notes
Session 10

Date:
Location:

Growth Assignments for Session 10:

Scripture for Memorization:

Session 11 Date:

Session 11 Location:

Growth Assignments and Additional Notes

Growth Assignments and Additional Notes

Counseling Notes
Session 11

Date:
Location:

Growth Assignments for Session 11:

Scripture for Memorization:

Session 12 Date:

Session 12 Location:

Growth Assignments and Additional Notes

Growth Assignments and Additional Notes

Counseling Notes
Session 12

Date:
Location:

Growth Assignments for the Path Forward:

Growth Assignments and Additional Notes

Growth Assignments and Additional Notes

Reflect on Your Recent Growth in Grace

PUT OFF	PUT ON
Ungodly thoughts, words, and actions	Godly thoughts, words, and actions

PUT OFF	PUT ON
Ungodly thoughts, words, and actions	Godly thoughts, words, and actions

PUT OFF	PUT ON
Ungodly thoughts, words, and actions	Godly thoughts, words, and actions

PUT OFF	PUT ON
Ungodly thoughts, words, and actions	Godly thoughts, words, and actions

PUT OFF	PUT ON
Ungodly thoughts, words, and actions	Godly thoughts, words, and actions

Topical Scripture Index

Adultery
Genesis 39:6–21
Exodus 20:14
2 Samuel 11:2–5
Psalm 51
Proverbs 6:20–7:27
Proverbs 9:17–18
Proverbs 23:26–28
Matthew 5:27–32
1 Corinthians 6:9–11
Hebrews 13:4

Alcohol Use
Genesis 9:20–23
Proverbs 20:1
Proverbs 21:17
Proverbs 23:19–21
Proverbs 23:29–35
Isaiah 28:1–8
Luke 21:34–36
1 Corinthians 5:11
1 Corinthians 6:9–11
Ephesians 5:15–18

Anger
Psalm 7:11
Proverbs 14:16–17
Proverbs 15:1
Proverbs 22:24–25
Proverbs 29:22
Proverbs 30:33
Matthew 5:21–22
Galatians 5:19–25
Ephesians 4:26
James 1:19–20

Anxiety (*See* Fear)

Assurance of Salvation (*See also* Salvation)
Job 19:25–27
Romans 8:16–17
2 Timothy 1:12
1 Peter 1:3–5
1 John 3:1–3
1 John 4:13–16
1 John 5:13

Bad Memories
Isaiah 43:18–19
Isaiah 65:17–19
2 Corinthians 5:16–19
Philippians 3:12–14
Philippians 4:8–9
Revelation 21:3–4

Besetting Sins (*See* Life-Dominating Sins)

Biblical Change Process (*See also* Progressive Sanctification)
Romans 12:1–2
2 Corinthians 4:16–18
Ephesians 4:11–16
Philippians 1:6
2 Timothy 3:14–17
Titus 2:11–14
James 1:2–4
2 Peter 1:3–9

Bitterness
Genesis 37
Proverbs 10:12
Proverbs 10:18
Proverbs 26:24–26
Matthew 5:43–48
Galatians 5:15–19
Ephesians 4:31–32
Hebrews 12:14–15
1 John 2:9–11
1 John 4:20–21

Blaming Others
Genesis 3:12–13
Proverbs 19:3
Proverbs 28:13–14
Matthew 7:1–5
Romans 2:1–3
Galatians 6:1–8

Child Training (*See also* Parenting)
Deuteronomy 6:4–9
Proverbs 1:8–9
Proverbs 13:24
Proverbs 22:6
Proverbs 23:13–14
Ephesians 6:4
Colossians 3:21
Hebrews 12:4–11

Children
Genesis 17:1–7
2 Samuel 12:18–23
Psalm 127:3–5
Proverbs 17:6
Acts 2:37–39
Acts 16:30–34

Church Life
Ezekiel 34:1–16
Acts 20:28–32
Romans 12:4–8
1 Corinthians 1:10–17
1 Corinthians 12:1–31
Ephesians 2:19–22

Ephesians 4:1–16
1 Timothy 5:17–20
Hebrews 10:23–25
Hebrews 13:17

Comfort
Psalm 23
Psalm 89:1–8
Psalm 103:8–18
Psalm 139:1–12
Isaiah 40:10–11
John 10:27–29
Romans 8:28–39
2 Corinthians 1:3–7
2 Corinthians 12:7–10
Revelation 21:1–4

Communication
Proverbs 10:19
Proverbs 12:18
Proverbs 13:3
Proverbs 15:1–4
Proverbs 17:27–28
Proverbs 19:9
Matthew 12:33–37
Ephesians 4:15–29
James 1:19–21
James 3:1–12

Conscience
Acts 24:14–16
Romans 2:14–15
Romans 13:3–5
1 Timothy 1:3–7
Hebrews 9:6–14
Hebrews 10:19–22
1 Peter 3:15–16

Contentment
2 Kings 20:12–19
Proverbs 15:16–17
Proverbs 16:16–17
Proverbs 23:4–5
Ecclesiastes 5:8–17
Habakkuk 3:17–19
Matthew 6:19–33
Mark 4:1–20
Philippians 4:11–13
1 Timothy 6:6–10

Covetousness
Exodus 20:17
Deuteronomy 5:21
Psalm 10:2–3
Mark 7:21–23
Luke 12:13–21
Romans 13:9–10
1 Corinthians 10:6–7
Ephesians 5:5
Colossians 3:5–6
1 Timothy 6:9–10

Death
Psalm 23:4–6
John 3:14–18
John 11:17–27
Romans 8:35–39
1 Corinthians 15:12–57

Philippians 1:21–26
1 Thessalonians 4:13–18
2 Timothy 4:7–8
1 John 5:11–12
Revelation 21:1–4

Decision Making
Joshua 24:14–27
1 Kings 18:16–39
Romans 12:1–2
Hebrews 3:7–11
Hebrews 11:24–26

Depression
Genesis 4:6–7
Psalm 32:1–5
Psalm 42
Proverbs 28:13
Isaiah 40
2 Corinthians 4:7–18
2 Corinthians 11:23–28

Despair (*See* Hopelessness)

Discipline
Psalm 94:12–14
Proverbs 3:11–12
Proverbs 6:23
Proverbs 12:1
Proverbs 13:24
Proverbs 23:13
Proverbs 29:15–17
Ephesians 6:4
1 Timothy 4:7–10
Hebrews 12:5–11

Divorce
Genesis 2:22–24
Malachi 2:13–16
Matthew 5:31–32
Matthew 18:15–18
Matthew 19:3–9
Romans 7:1–3
Romans 12:16–18
1 Corinthians 7:10–16

Doubts
Genesis 18:10–14
Exodus 3–4
Matthew 11:1–7
Matthew 28:17–20
Luke 24:36–42
John 20:24–29
James 1:5–8
Jude 1:22

Eating Problems
Romans 12:1–2
Romans 14:15–18
1 Corinthians 6:19–20
1 Corinthians 10:13
1 Corinthians 10:31

End of Life (*See* Death)

Envy
Psalm 37:1–3
Proverbs 14:30
Proverbs 23:17
Romans 1:28–32
1 Corinthians 3:1–9
1 Corinthians 13:4–7
Galatians 5:19–26
Titus 3:3–7
James 3:14–4:10
1 Peter 2:1–2

Eternity
John 10:27–30
John 11:17–26
John 14:1–6
Romans 8:35–39
1 Corinthians 15:12–28
2 Corinthians 5:1–8
1 Thessalonians 4:13–18
1 Peter 1:3–9
1 John 3:1–2
Revelation 21:1–4

Evil
Romans 8:5–8
Romans 13:12–14
Galatians 5:16–21
Ephesians 2:1–3
Titus 2:11–12
1 Peter 1:14–16
1 Peter 2:11–12

Faith (*See* Faithfulness)

Faithfulness
Psalm 28:7–8
Psalm 36:5–9
Psalm 46:1–3
Psalm 62:5–8
Psalm 73:23–24
Isaiah 43:1–3
Lamentations 3:22–24
Matthew 6:25–34
Matthew 14:22–33
Hebrews 11

Fear
Psalm 27:1
Psalm 56:3–4
Matthew 6:19–34
Matthew 10:28–30
Matthew 14:22–33
Romans 8:12–15
Hebrews 13:5–6
1 John 4:18–21

Fear of People
Deuteronomy 1:16–17
Psalm 27:1
Psalm 56:4–11
Psalm 118:5–9
Proverbs 29:25
Isaiah 51:7–8
Luke 12:4–5
Romans 8:31–39

Hebrews 13:6
1 Peter 3:13–17

Forgiveness
Psalm 86:4–7
Psalm 103:8–12
Isaiah 38:15–19
Luke 7:36–50
Luke 15:11–32
John 4:4–26
Romans 3:21–26
Romans 8:1–4
1 John 1:7–9
1 John 2:1–2

Gossip (*See also* The Tongue)
Psalm 19:12–14
Psalm 34:11–14
Proverbs 8:6–8
Proverbs 10:19
Proverbs 11:11–13
Proverbs 13:3
Proverbs 15:28
Proverbs 18:13
Ephesians 4:25–29
James 3:1–12

Greed
Proverbs 1:8–19
Proverbs 15:27
Proverbs 28:25
Ecclesiastes 5:10–11
Matthew 6:24
Luke 12:13–21
1 Timothy 6:6–10
Hebrews 13:5
1 John 2:15–17

Grief
Psalm 31:9–10
Psalm 34:15–18
Psalm 147:2–3
Isaiah 53:3
2 Corinthians 1:3–5
1 Thessalonians 4:13–18
Revelation 21:1–4

Guilt (*See* Forgiveness)

Hardship (*See also* Trials)
Job 1–2
Psalm 27:5–6
John 9:1–3
Romans 8:18–30
1 Corinthians 10:13
2 Corinthians 1:3–11
2 Corinthians 4:7–18
2 Corinthians 12:7–10
James 1:2–4
1 Peter 1:3–9

Hate
Leviticus 19:16–17
Proverbs 10:12
Proverbs 10:18

Proverbs 26:24–26
Matthew 5:43–48
Ephesians 4:31–32
Hebrews 12:14–15
1 John 2:9–11
1 John 3:11–20
1 John 4:20–21

Headship and Submission (*See also* Submission to Authority)
Genesis 2:18–25
Proverbs 31:10–31
Matthew 12:24–30
Ephesians 5:22–32
Colossians 3:18–19
1 Peter 3:1–7

Homosexuality
Genesis 18:20–21
Genesis 19
Leviticus 18:22
Romans 1:18–32
1 Corinthians 6:9–10
2 Peter 2:4–10

Hopelessness
Psalm 46
Psalm 146:3–10
Lamentations 3:31–32
Romans 15:12–13
1 Corinthians 10:13
2 Corinthians 9:8
Ephesians 3:20–21
1 Thessalonians 1:2–5
Hebrews 6:19–20
1 Peter 1:3–5

Humility
Psalm 18:24–27
Psalm 25:8–10
Proverbs 3:34
Proverbs 11:2
Zechariah 9:9
Matthew 11:28–30
Romans 12:14–16
Philippians 2:3–11
James 4:6–10
1 Peter 5:5–6

Identity in Christ
John 1:9–13
Romans 6:1–14
Galatians 2:19–21
Galatians 3:25–29
Ephesians 1:3–14
Colossians 3:1–4
1 Peter 2:4–10

Imitating Jesus
John 13:12–17
John 15:9–11
1 Corinthians 10:31–11:1
Ephesians 4:22–24
Ephesians 5:1–2
Colossians 3:9–11
1 Thessalonians 1:6–7

1 Peter 2:18–23
1 John 2:4–6
1 John 3:2–3

Laziness
Proverbs 6:6–11
Proverbs 10:5
Proverbs 12:11
Proverbs 15:19
Proverbs 19:15
Proverbs 20:4
Proverbs 24:30–34
Matthew 25:14–30
1 Corinthians 10:31
2 Thessalonians 3:11–12

Life-Dominating Sins
Romans 6:1–4
Romans 6:15–23
1 Corinthians 10:6–14
Colossians 3:1–15
Hebrews 2:14–18
Hebrews 3:12–13
Hebrews 4:14–16

Loneliness
Psalm 25:16–18
Psalm 102:1–12
Psalm 139:7–12
Isaiah 41:8–10
Matthew 28:18–20
Romans 8:31–38
1 John 4:13–16

Loving God
Deuteronomy 6:4–7
Joshua 22:5
Matthew 22:37–39
John 14:23–24
2 Corinthians 5:14–15

Loving Others
Matthew 22:34–40
John 13:31–35
John 15:12–17
Romans 12:9–10
Romans 13:8–10
Galatians 5:13–15
1 Peter 1:22–25
1 Peter 4:7–9
1 John 3:11–18
1 John 4:7–12

Lust (*See also* Pornography)
Genesis 3:6–7
Exodus 20:17
Matthew 5:27–30
Romans 13:12–14
Galatians 5:16–17
Ephesians 2:1–3
Titus 2:11–12
1 Peter 1:13–16
1 Peter 2:11–12

Marriage
Genesis 2:18–25
Exodus 34:13–16

Deuteronomy 7:3–4
Joshua 23:12–13
Nehemiah 13:23–27
Proverbs 31:10–31
2 Corinthians 6:14–16
Ephesians 5:22–33
Colossians 3:18–19
1 Peter 3:1–7

Obedience

Psalm 1
Psalm 119:1–8
Matthew 7:24–27
Luke 11:27–28
John 14:15
John 15:10–17
James 1:22–25
1 John 2:3–6
1 John 5:2–3
2 John 6

Overcoming Sin and Temptation (*See also* Temptation)

Proverbs 4:14–15
Matthew 4:1–11
Romans 6:15–18
1 Corinthians 10:6–13
Galatians 5:16–26
Ephesians 6:10–17
Philippians 2:12–13
James 1:13–16
1 Peter 5:8–9
2 Peter 2:9–10

Parenting (*See also* Child Training)

Deuteronomy 6:4–9
Psalm 103:13
Psalm 127:3–5
Proverbs 1:8–9
Proverbs 13:24
Proverbs 29:15
Isaiah 66:13
Ephesians 6:4
Colossians 3:21
Hebrews 12:7–11

Patience (*See also* Waiting for God)

1 Samuel 13:8–14
Psalm 37:5–9
Psalm 40:1–3
Proverbs 25:15
Matthew 18:23–35
Galatians 5:22–23
Colossians 3:12–14
Hebrews 6:11–15
James 5:7–11

Peace

Psalm 4:8
Psalm 85:8
Isaiah 26:3–4
Matthew 11:28–30
John 14:25–27
Romans 5:1–2

Romans 8:5–8
Philippians 4:4–8

Perfectionism
Psalm 18:30–32
Matthew 23:25–26
2 Corinthians 5:21
Philippians 3:4–11
Hebrews 5:7–10
Hebrews 10:11–14
James 1:23–25

Pornography (*See also* Lust)
Job 31:1–4
Matthew 5:27–30
Matthew 15:17–20
Romans 6:15–19
1 Corinthians 6:12–20
Galatians 5:16–24
Ephesians 5:1–3
Colossians 3:5–7
1 Thessalonians 4:1–8

Prayer
Psalm 50:14–15
Jeremiah 29:12–13
Matthew 6:9–13
Matthew 7:7–11
Matthew 11:28–30
John 15:5–8
Philippians 4:6–7
1 Thessalonians 5:16–18
James 5:14–16
1 Peter 5:6–7

Pride
Psalm 10:2–4
Psalm 31:18–24
Proverbs 8:12–13
Proverbs 11:2
Proverbs 16:18–19
Proverbs 29:23
Isaiah 2:10–19
Isaiah 13:9–11
Mark 7:20–23
1 John 2:15–17

Progressive Sanctification (*See also* Biblical Change Process)
Psalm 119:11
John 14:25–26
John 15:1–8
Romans 12:1–2
Philippians 2:12–13
Philippians 3:12–14
1 Timothy 4:7–8
Hebrews 12:1–2
2 Peter 1:5–11
1 John 2:3–6

Providence of God
Deuteronomy 31:7–8
Psalm 103:19

Sexual Issues
Proverbs 5:18–20
Matthew 5:27–28
1 Corinthians 6:9–20
1 Corinthians 7:3–5
Colossians 3:5–7
1 Thessalonians 4:3–6
Hebrews 13:4
2 Peter 2:4–10

Speech (*See* Communication, The Tongue)

Submission to Authority (*See also* Headship and Submission)
Romans 13:1–7
Ephesians 5:22–24
Colossians 3:18–25
1 Thessalonians 5:12–13
Titus 3:1–3
Hebrews 13:17
1 Peter 2:13–25
1 Peter 5:5–7

Temptation (*See also* Overcoming Sin and Temptation)
Genesis 3:1–7
Proverbs 1:10
Matthew 4:1–11
Matthew 26:40–41
2 Corinthians 11:14–15
Ephesians 6:10–18
James 1:13–15
1 Peter 5:8–9

The Tongue (*See also* Gossip)
Psalm 34:11–14
Proverbs 8:6–8
Proverbs 12:18
Proverbs 17:28
Proverbs 18:13
Proverbs 19:9
Proverbs 21:23
Proverbs 29:20
James 1:19–21
James 3:1–12

Trials (*See also* Hardship)
Deuteronomy 8:2–5
Psalm 27:5–6
Psalm 119:67–68
John 9:1–3
Romans 5:3–5
Romans 8:28–30
2 Corinthians 4:7–12
Philippians 1:12–26
James 1:2–4
1 Peter 1:3–7

Trust
Joshua 1:1–9
Psalm 27
Psalm 37:1–7
Psalm 91:1–2

Proverbs 3:5–6
Jeremiah 17:7–8
Jeremiah 32:26–27
Lamentations 3:22–24
Matthew 8:23–27

Waiting for God (*See also* Patience)
Psalm 34:15–18
Psalm 105:1–4
Isaiah 55:6–9
Philippians 4:4–13
1 Thessalonians 5:17–18
Hebrews 4:14–16
James 1:2–8
1 Peter 5:6–7

Work
Genesis 2:5–15
Proverbs 6:6–11
Proverbs 10:5
Proverbs 24:30–34
Ecclesiastes 5:12
1 Corinthians 10:31
Ephesians 4:28
Colossians 3:17
2 Thessalonians 3:6–12
1 Timothy 5:8

Worry (*See* Fear)

Worthless Feelings (*See* Self-Focus)

Association of Certified Biblical Counselors

Since 1976, the Association of Certified Biblical Counselors (ACBC) has been training and certifying biblical counselors to ensure excellence in the counseling room by faithfulness to the Word of God. We offer a comprehensive biblical counseling certification program that is rigorous, but attainable by even the busiest pastor or church member. Our certification process is made up of three phases: learning, exams and application, and supervision.

ACBC has grown from a handful of individuals to thousands of certified counselors all around the world. For over forty years we have been pursuing excellence in biblical counseling. We have had six executive directors of the organization: Dr. Bob Smith, Dr. Howard Eyrich, Rev. Bill Goode, Rev. Randy Patten, Dr. Heath Lambert, and Dr. Dale Johnson.

Every Christian is called to speak the truth in love to one another. ACBC trains Christians in their gospel responsibility to be disciple-makers and to build up the body of Christ. This training is accomplished through conferences and events throughout the world.

For more information about ACBC and biblical counseling resources, visit www.biblicalcounseling.com.

Published in Partnership with ACBC

"Wow! What a needed resource for single men and women. Dating can be one of the most confusing times in a single person's life, and we desperately need solid biblical guidance in this area. Thank you, Sean and Spencer, for giving us this incredibly practical and biblical book on dating. We highly recommend it!"

—**Kristen Clark and Bethany Baird**, Founders, Girl-Defined Ministries

"Engagement is an exhilarating step toward the unknown with someone you're still getting to know. Where can a couple get wise counsel for a season that ricochets, almost daily, between sparkling anticipation and disorienting discussion? The answer is two guys and a book. . . . You will come away packed with fresh faith, enriched by practical insights, and uniquely prepared for the magnificent journey toward marriage!"

—**Dave Harvey**, Executive Director, Sojourn Network

Published in Partnership with ACBC

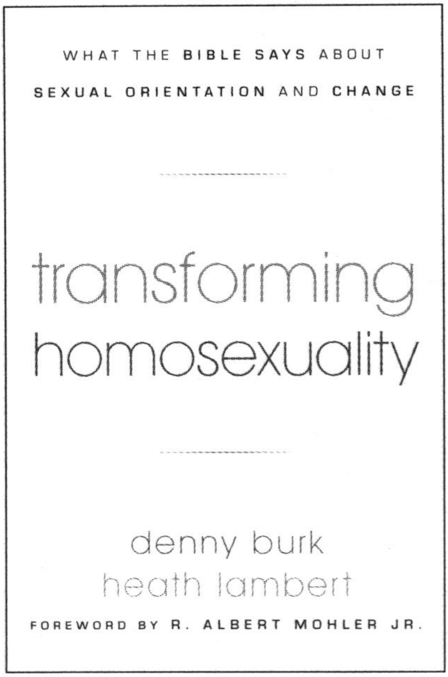

Challenging misconceptions on all sides of the homosexuality debate, Burk and Lambert show how a biblical view of same-sex orientation, temptation, and desire gives hope for profound personal change.

"A bold and provocative book. . . . But predominantly a loving book that seeks to help people with unwanted homosexual desires be transformed by the full knowledge that God's grace for us in Christ is sufficient for all our various struggles."

—**Rosaria Butterfield**, Author, *The Secret Thoughts of an Unlikely Convert*

New from P&R

Commonplace, familiar sins are dangerous—they sneak in and become habits! Rush Witt defines these subtle sins that seem so unkillable, then shows how change is possible through Christ.

"Rush Witt's *Diehard Sins* is a clarion call for holiness that also provides us with meaningful and theologically rich resources to fight indwelling sin. This book is a careful and refreshing resource that every Christian should read."

—**R. Albert Mohler Jr.**, President, The Southern Baptist Theological Seminary

Counseling Classics from P&R

Examine the expectations that you, your future spouse, and God himself have for marriage, while addressing and overcoming potential conflicts.

"The staple of my pre-marriage counseling for many years. . . . Using this book . . . helps couples to identify the pressure points in their relationships as well as the path forward for resolving the conflicts that occur again and again."

—**Tedd Tripp**, President, Shepherding the Heart Ministries

Counseling Classics from P&R

"Far and away the best material on anger I have read, thoroughly biblical and immensely practical. Jones does a masterful job of helping us identify anger in our lives, then gives us biblical steps for uprooting it. Every Christian ought to prayerfully read this book and apply its teaching."

—**Jerry Bridges**, author, *The Pursuit of Holiness*

"Most of us find it all too easy to use words like *hurt*, *frustrated*, and *troubled* to conceal the fact that we are often controlled by sinful anger. This book cuts through this disguise, exposes our bondage to anger, and marks a clear path to peace and freedom."

—**Ken Sande**, President, Peacemaker Ministries

Counseling Classics from P&R

When we are struggling to grow in Christ, it's time to search our hearts for idolatry. Using personal examples, Bigney shows us how to recognize and root out hidden idols.

"Brad has thought a lot about the insidiousness of idolatry in today's culture. He has done a thorough job of showing us how modern-day idols are both offensive to God and grace-robbing to the believer. This book will cause you to consider your own heart in terms of what you really want and live for. It will also help you to minister to others who are suffering or caught in sin that hinders them from the freedom we have in the gospel."

—**Garrett Higbee**, President and Founder, Twelve Stones Ministries